HUMAN
CONNECTIONS

BEYOND SALES, MARKETING
TECHNOLOGIES, AND
CUSTOMER PSYCHOLOGY

BY TONI URRUTIA

WWW.TONIURRUTIA.COM

The State of Marketing: Customer Psychology, Technology, and Art
Copyright © 2023 by Toni Urrutia

ISBN: 9798394305962
Imprint: Independently published

For permission requests, please contact the publisher at:
Email: books@toniurrutia.com
Phone: +1 (408) 502-6533
Address: 92 Brighton Ct, Daly City, CA 94015
Website: www.toniurrutia.com

CONTENTS

TECHNOLOGY'S INFLUENCE ON MARKETING

While some marketing principles have become obsolete because of technology, many core principles such as understanding your audience, creating value, building relationships, and measuring results have persisted and remain essential in the digital age.

Several marketing principles have persisted through all the technological changes in the marketing landscape, including:

- **Understanding your target audience**: No matter what technology or platform is being used, it's important to understand who your target audience is and what they want or need. This involves conducting research to understand their demographics, interests, behaviors, and pain points, and tailoring your marketing efforts accordingly.
- **Creating value for customers**: Providing value to customers has always been a fundamental principle of marketing. This can involve creating high-quality products or services, offering exceptional customer service, or providing relevant and helpful content or information.
- **Building relationships with customers**: Building strong relationships with customers has always been an important aspect of marketing. This can involve engaging with customers on social media, responding to their feedback and concerns, and offering personalized recommendations or promotions based on their behavior or preferences.
- **Measuring and analyzing results**: Measuring the effectiveness of marketing campaigns and analyzing the results to inform future efforts has always been an essential part of marketing. This involves using data and analytics to track key performance indicators (KPIs) such as website traffic, conversions, and customer engagement.

On the other hand, some marketing principles have become obsolete or less relevant because of technology, such as:

- **Interruption-based marketing**: Traditional interruption-based marketing tactics such as cold calling and direct mail are becoming less effective in the digital age, as consumers increasingly block or ignore these types of messages.

- **Mass marketing**: With the ability to target specific audiences through digital channels, the one-size-fits-all approach of mass marketing is becoming less effective. Personalization and targeting are becoming increasingly important in the marketing landscape.

- **Static content**: With the rise of social media and other interactive digital channels, static content such as print ads and billboards are becoming less effective. Engaging and interactive content such as videos, live streams, and augmented reality experiences are becoming more important.

- **Short-term thinking**: With the ability to track and analyze data in real-time, marketers can increasingly take a long-term view of marketing, focusing on building relationships with customers over time rather than just driving short-term sales.

Event-driven technological marketing is a high margin, high risk, high reward opportunity because it leverages technology to deliver personalized experiences to consumers in real-time. By using real-time data and advanced algorithms, businesses can analyze consumer behavior and preferences and then deliver customized messaging and experiences that are relevant to the individual consumer.

One of the reasons why event-driven technological marketing is high margin is that it allows businesses to better target their audience and drive higher conversion rates. By analyzing consumer behavior and preferences in real-time, businesses can create highly personalized campaigns that are more likely to resonate with the target audience. This, in turn, can lead to higher conversion rates and ultimately higher profits.

However, with the potential for high rewards also comes high risks. One of the main risks of event-driven technological marketing is that it relies heavily on the technology being used to collect and analyze data. If the technology is not reliable or if there is a data breach, businesses could potentially lose access to critical customer data or even face legal consequences. Additionally, the use of advanced algorithms and real-time data analysis requires highly skilled professionals, which can be costly and difficult to find.

Despite these risks, the potential rewards of event-driven technological marketing are significant. One example of a successful event-driven marketing campaign is the "Share a Coke" campaign, which was launched by Coca-Cola in 2011. The campaign allowed customers to personalize Coke bottles with their names, and the brand used social media and other digital platforms to encourage customers to share photos of their personalized bottles. The campaign was a massive success, generating over 500,000 photos shared on social media and a 7% increase in sales.

Another example of a successful event-driven marketing campaign is the "Black Friday" sales event, which takes place annually in the United States on the day after Thanksgiving. Retailers use this event to drive high-volume sales by offering significant discounts and promotions. By leveraging real-time data and advanced algorithms, retailers can identify which products are likely to be most popular and then target their promotions to specific demographics or geographic regions.

event-driven technological marketing presents a high margin, high risk, high reward opportunity for businesses. By leveraging real-time data and advanced algorithms, companies can create highly personalized campaigns that are more likely to resonate with their target audience, leading to higher conversion rates and ultimately higher profits. However, businesses must also be aware of the potential risks involved, including reliance on technology and the need for highly skilled professionals.

Super Bowl marketing can be classified as a type of event marketing or experiential marketing. Brands use Super Bowl commercials as an opportunity to create a memorable and engaging experience for viewers, often using humor, emotion, or celebrity endorsements to capture the attention of the audience. Super Bowl commercials are highly sought after due to the massive audience and cultural significance of the event, which makes it a unique opportunity for brands to make a splash and increase brand awareness.

There have been several famous examples of using high technology in conjunction with Super Bowl ads and commercials. Here are a few:

1. Coca-Cola's "It's Beautiful" commercial (2014) - This ad used technology to showcase the diversity of America by featuring people from different cultures and backgrounds singing "America the Beautiful" in different languages.
2. Oreo's "Dunk in the Dark" tweet (2013) - When the power went out during the Super Bowl, Oreo quickly tweeted a picture of an Oreo cookie in the dark with the caption "You can still dunk in the dark." The tweet went viral and showcased the power of real-time marketing.
3. Amazon's Alexa ad (2018) - Amazon used its Super Bowl ad to introduce its Alexa technology and showcase its capabilities, including ordering pizza and playing music.
4. Doritos' "The Best Part" commercial (2010) - This ad used technology to create a 3D effect, with a man's hand reaching through the screen to grab a Dorito chip.
5. Hyundai's "Smaht Pahk" ad (2020) - This ad used high-tech features like automatic parking assist and voice recognition to showcase the new Hyundai Sonata.
6. Coinbase ran a Super Bowl ad in 2022, which featured a QR code that viewers could scan to receive $1 million worth of cryptocurrency. While it needs to be clarified how successful the ad was in terms of driving new cryptocurrency users or transactions, it did generate significant buzz and media coverage. Some experts have praised the ad as a creative use of QR code technology in advertising, while others criticized it as a shallow attempt to cash in on the hype around the Super Bowl. Ultimately, the success of the ad likely depends on Coinbase's overall marketing goals and metrics for success.

The examples show how brands have used high technology to create memorable and engaging experiences for viewers during the Super Bowl, often with the goal of increasing brand awareness and driving sales.

Artificial intelligence (AI) is transforming how marketers engage in growth hacking by providing powerful tools to automate and optimize various aspects of the process. One of the key ways AI is changing growth hacking is by helping marketers analyze large amounts of data quickly and accurately. By using AI-powered tools, marketers can identify patterns and trends in data that would otherwise go unnoticed, allowing them to make informed decisions and take action faster.

Another way AI is changing growth hacking is by enabling marketers to personalize their approach to each individual customer. By using machine learning algorithms, marketers can analyze a customer's behavior, preferences, and needs to create targeted, personalized campaigns that are more likely to convert. This approach allows marketers to deliver the right message to the right customer at the right time, increasing engagement and ultimately driving growth.

AI is also changing the way marketers test and optimize their campaigns. By using AI-powered A/B testing tools, marketers can quickly and accurately test different variations of their campaigns to see which performs best. This allows them to make data-driven decisions and optimize their campaigns for maximum impact.

AI is revolutionizing how marketers engage in growth hacking by providing powerful tools to automate and optimize various aspects of the process. As AI technology continues to evolve, we can expect to see even more innovative and effective ways for marketers to use AI to drive growth and achieve their goals, especially when it comes to identifying parts of a product that can incorporate and integrate ("bake in") growth hacking features.

BAKED-IN GROWTH-HACKS

Artificial intelligence (AI) is transforming the way product heads, leads, and managers approach growth hacking by assisting them in identifying critical components of a product that can be used to "bake in" growth hacking strategies. AI-powered tools can analyze vast amounts of data on customer behavior, preferences, and usage patterns to identify areas of a product that can be optimized for growth.

For example, AI-powered analytics tools can identify the features of a product that are most popular with customers and highlight potential areas for improvement. This information can be used to design new features or improve existing ones that are most likely to resonate with customers and drive growth.

AI can also assist in creating personalized user experiences that encourage growth. By analyzing data on user behavior and preferences, AI-powered tools can create personalized recommendations and content that encourage users to engage more deeply with a product. This not only enhances the user experience, but also increases the likelihood of retention and growth.

In addition, AI can help product heads, leads, and managers identify opportunities for growth beyond the product itself. For example, AI-powered tools can analyze data on customer interactions with social media, email marketing campaigns, and other channels to identify areas where growth hacking strategies can be applied.

In summary, AI is transforming how product heads, leads, and managers approach growth hacking by providing powerful tools to analyze customer behavior, personalize experiences, and identify growth opportunities. By leveraging AI, product teams can "bake in" growth hacking strategies into their products and create experiences that not only engage users but also drive growth.

AI-marketing is a relatively new category of marketing that involves the use of artificial intelligence (AI) technologies to optimize marketing processes and deliver more targeted and personalized messaging to customers. AI-marketing encompasses a range of strategies and techniques, including data analysis, predictive analytics, natural language processing (NLP), machine learning, and chatbots.

AI-marketing can be applied across a range of marketing categories, including digital marketing, social media marketing, email marketing, content marketing, and more. Its applications are diverse, from improving customer segmentation and targeting to automating routine marketing tasks, generating personalized content, and predicting future trends and behavior.

AI-macustomer assistancerketing is an emerging field that has the potential to transform the way businesses approach marketing by enabling more data-driven and personalized approaches to engagement and communication. As AI technology continues to advance, it is likely to play an increasingly important role in the future of marketing.

AI (Artificial Intelligence) has had a significant impact on marketing in recent years, and its influence is only expected to grow in the future. Here are some ways in which AI has changed and affected marketing:

1. Personalization: AI has enabled marketers to personalize their campaigns and messaging based on individual customer preferences, behavior, and data. This helps to improve customer engagement, loyalty, and conversions.
2. Automation: AI has made it possible to automate various marketing tasks, such as lead scoring, content creation, email marketing, and social media management. This helps to increase efficiency and productivity while reducing costs.
3. Predictive Analytics: AI-powered predictive analytics allows marketers to make data-driven decisions about their campaigns and strategies. This helps identify patterns, trends, and insights that can inform marketing decisions and improve performance.
4. Chatbots: AI-powered chatbots have become increasingly popular in customer service and support, providing instant and personalized assistance to customers 24/7.

5. Search Optimization: RankBrain is a machine learning-based search engine algorithm developed by Google to improve the accuracy and relevance of search results. It was confirmed by Google in October 2015 and is considered one of the three most significant ranking factors in Google's algorithm, along with links and content. RankBrain uses artificial intelligence and natural language processing to learn and interpret user search queries, particularly those that are long-tail or infrequently used. It tries to understand the meaning behind queries and then maps them to entities or clusters of words that are relevant to the search. Essentially, RankBrain helps Google to better process and understand search queries, providing users more effective and satisfactory results.
6. Voice Search: AI-powered virtual assistants, such as Siri and Alexa, have changed the way consumers search for information and interact with brands, which impacts SEO and content strategies.

AI has enabled marketers to be more data-driven, efficient, and personalized in their approach. By leveraging AI technology, marketers can better understand their audience, optimize their campaigns, and deliver more relevant and engaging experiences to their customers.

Figure 1 - AI-video Apps

App Platform	Pricing	Free Trial	Special Features	Marketing Use Cases
Animoto	Starting at $5/month	Yes	AI-powered video creation, customizable styles and templates, drag-and-drop interface	Social media marketing, product demos, event promotion
Vidyard	Starting at $15/month	Yes	AI-powered personalization, advanced analytics, and integrations with CRM systems	Sales enablement, customer testimonials, internal training
Wibbitz	Starting at $1,000/mo.	Yes	AI-powered video creation, text-to-video capability, customizable templates, integrations with CMS platforms	News production, content marketing, e-learning
Lumen5	Starting at $49/mo.	Yes	AI-powered video creation, customizable themes, integrations with stock image libraries	Social media marketing, explainer videos, educational content
Magisto	Starting at $4.99/mo.	Yes	AI-powered video creation, customizable templates, music library, social media scheduling	Event promotion, product marketing, brand storytelling
Moovly	Starting at $49/mo.	Yes	AI-powered video creation, customizable templates, and graphics, voice-over recording	E-learning, content marketing, product demos
StoryTap	Contact for Pricing	Yes	AI-powered video creation, customizable templates, influencer marketing capabilities	User-generated content, brand advocacy, social media marketing
Rocketium	Starting at $49/month	Yes	AI-powered video creation, customizable templates and graphics, integrations with stock image libraries	Social media marketing, product demos, event promotion
Hippo Video	Starting at $15/month	Yes	AI-powered personalization, integrations with sales and marketing tools, video engagement analytics	Sales enablement, customer testimonials, email marketing
Biteable	Starting at $19/month	Yes	AI-powered video creation, customizable templates, animated infographics, integrations with social media platforms	Social media marketing, explainer videos, product demos

AI is increasingly being used to enhance video marketing strategies for businesses. With AI, companies can gain insights into customer behavior, deliver personalized content, and maximize video ROI. AI helps marketers deliver the right message to the right customer at the right time by creating more personalized content. Through different algorithms, AI enables businesses to analyze large amounts of data in real-time and create hyper-personalized content and experiences that target audiences more effectively. This leads to more engaged and loyal customers who feel that the brand truly understands and cares about them, which can also create a community around the brand. AI is transforming video marketing by delivering personalized customer experiences and engaging audiences.

BOOKS

1. "Video Marketing Strategy: Harness the Power of Online Video to Drive Brand Growth" by Jon Mowat
2. "The Art of Video Marketing: How to Create Videos That Engage and Grow Your Audience" by Jace Vernon
3. "The AI Marketing Canvas: A Five-Stage Road Map to Implementing Artificial Intelligence in Marketing" by Andrea Fryrear

WEBSITES

1. Vidyard Blog: A great resource for video marketing tips and insights, with a focus on the use of AI and personalization in video marketing.
2. Wibbitz Blog: An excellent source of information on AI-driven video production and content creation, with tips and tutorials for marketers.
3. ReelSEO: A comprehensive resource for video marketing news, best practices, and insights, including a section on AI and machine learning in video marketing.

Agile marketing is a buzzword that has been gaining popularity in the marketing world for several years now. At its core, agile marketing is a methodology that allows marketing teams to respond quickly to market and customer needs changes, test and optimize their marketing strategies, and ultimately achieve better results. However, agile marketing is not just for large enterprises with big budgets and dedicated marketing teams. Solopreneurs can also benefit from adopting agile marketing practices.

Agile marketing is based on the principles of agile software development, which emphasizes collaboration, flexibility, and adaptability. This methodology can help solopreneurs stay ahead of the curve and make the most of limited resources. Agile marketing is a great way for solopreneurs to stay agile, stay competitive, and keep up with the ever-changing landscape of online marketing.

The first step to adopting agile marketing is to understand the principles that underlie it. Agile marketing focuses on collaboration, experimentation, and continuous improvement. Agile marketing teams work together in short sprints, testing and refining their strategies along the way. This approach allows them to make rapid progress and pivot quickly if needed.

Solopreneurs can apply the same principles to their own marketing efforts. For example, they can set short-term goals, experiment with different strategies, and use data to measure and improve their results. They can also leverage agile marketing tools, such as project management software, A/B testing tools, and analytics platforms to help them make informed decisions and stay on track.

Agile marketing is especially beneficial for solopreneurs because it allows them to work more efficiently and effectively. By focusing on short-term goals and iterative improvements, solopreneurs can make progress faster and achieve better results. They can also avoid wasting time and resources on strategies that aren't working, and instead focus on those that are.

Another advantage of agile marketing for solopreneurs is that it encourages a mindset of continuous learning and improvement. Agile marketing teams constantly experiment and test new ideas, which allows them to learn from their mistakes and improve over time. Solopreneurs can adopt the same approach by embracing a growth mindset and being open to trying new things.

Agile marketing is a powerful methodology that can help solopreneurs stay competitive in the fast-paced world of online marketing. By adopting agile marketing principles and tools, solopreneurs can work more efficiently, experiment with different strategies, and achieve better results. If you're a solopreneur looking to take your marketing to the next level, then it's time to embrace agile marketing and start experimenting with new ideas today.

Growth hacking is considered a kind of agile marketing because it shares many principles and practices with agile methodologies. Both growth hacking and agile marketing prioritize continuous experimentation, data-driven decision-making, and a flexible, iterative approach to marketing.

Agile marketing is an approach to marketing that takes its inspiration from agile software development methodologies. It emphasizes a flexible, iterative approach to marketing that is highly responsive to customer needs and feedback. Agile marketing involves breaking down marketing campaigns into small, manageable chunks called sprints, and then testing and iterating on those sprints to improve performance over time.

Growth hacking is a type of marketing that focuses on rapid experimentation and continuous improvement in order to achieve growth. Growth hackers use a variety of techniques, including A/B testing, social media marketing, and viral marketing, to rapidly test and iterate on marketing campaigns. The goal is to quickly identify what works and what doesn't, and then double down on the strategies that are most effective.

One of the key reasons why growth hacking is considered a kind of agile marketing is because both approaches emphasize rapid experimentation and continuous improvement. Both growth hackers and agile marketers are constantly testing and iterating on their campaigns to optimize performance and achieve their goals.

Another reason growth hacking is considered a kind of agile marketing is becathath approaches prioritize data-driven decision-making. Growth hackers and agile marketers alike use data to inform their decisions and to measure the impact of their campaigns. They use analytics tools to track key performance indicators (KPIs) and to gain insights into customer behavior, preferences, and needs.

Growth hacking and agile marketing also share a focus on customer-centricity. Both approaches emphasize the importance of understanding and meeting the needs of the customer. Growth hackers use techniques like A/B testing and customer surveys to gather feedback and insights into customer behavior, while agile marketers use tools like customer journey maps and user personas to gain a deeper understanding of their target audience.

While growth hacking is often associated with startups and tech companies, it is a mindset and approach that can be applied by any marketer or business owner. Solopreneurs, in particular, can benefit from adopting a growth hacking approach to marketing, as it allows them to quickly test and iterate on their marketing campaigns without the need for a large budget or team.

Growth hacking is considered a kind of agile marketing because it shares many of the same principles and practices. Both approaches prioritize rapid experimentation, data-driven decision-making, customer-centricity, and a flexible, iterative approach to marketing. By adopting a growth hacking mindset, solopreneurs and small business owners can quickly and effectively optimize their marketing campaigns for growth and success.

GROWTH HACKERS

Growth hacking has become a buzzword in the world of marketing, and for good reason. It has helped companies achieve exponential growth in a short amount of time. And while growth hacking is a relatively new term, the strategies and techniques used by growth hackers have been around for decades. In this chapter, we will explore some of the most prominent growth hackers and their strategies.

Sean Ellis

Sean Ellis is often referred to as the "father of growth hacking." He is the founder of GrowthHackers.com, a platform dedicated to helping businesses achieve growth through experimentation and optimization. Ellis is also known for popularizing the term "growth hacker."

Ellis has worked with companies such as Dropbox, Eventbrite, and LogMeIn, helping them achieve significant growth through his innovative strategies. One of his most famous growth hacking strategies is the "Growth Hacking Funnel," a framework for identifying the key metrics that drive growth.

Neil Patel is a well-known marketer and entrepreneur who has been named one of the top 10 marketers by Forbes. He is the co-founder of Crazy Egg, Hello Bar, and KISSmetrics, all of which have seen significant growth through his marketing strategies.

Patel is known for his content marketing and SEO expertise. He has published numerous blog posts and guides on these topics, helping businesses of all sizes improve their online visibility and traffic.

Andrew Chen is a general partner at Andreessen Horowitz, a Silicon Valley venture capital firm. He is also a well-known growth hacker who has worked with companies such as Uber, Dropbox, and Pinterest.

Chen is known for his expertise in user acquisition and retention. He has written extensively on these topics, sharing his insights and strategies with the broader marketing community. His blog, andrewchen.co, is a valuable resource for anyone looking to learn about growth hacking.

Brian Balfour is the founder and CEO of Reforge, a platform that provides growth-focused training and education for professionals. Balfour has also worked with companies such as HubSpot, KISSmetrics, and Groove to help them achieve significant growth.

Balfour is known for his expertise in growth strategy and optimization. He has developed frameworks such as the "3 stages of growth" and the "pirate metrics" to help businesses identify and prioritize the key metrics that drive growth.

Hiten Shah is a serial entrepreneur and the founder of several successful startups, including KISSmetrics, Crazy Egg, and FYI. He is known for his expertise in product development and growth.

Shah is a strong advocate of data-driven decision-making and has developed several tools to help businesses collect and analyze data.

He is also a prolific blogger and has written extensively on topics such as customer acquisition, retention, and product-market fit.

Conclusion

These are just a few of the most prominent growth hackers in the marketing community. They have all achieved significant success by focusing on data-driven experimentation, optimization, and innovation. And while their strategies may differ, they all share a common goal: to help businesses achieve exponential growth. Whether you are a solopreneur or part of a larger organization, there are valuable lessons to be learned from these growth hackers and their approaches to marketing. For more information and other learning resources, visit toniurrutia.com/growth.

VIRAL MARKETING

INTRODUCTION

Viral marketing has been around for decades, but the rise of the internet and social media has transformed this marketing technique into a powerful tool for businesses of all sizes. In recent years, the development of AI and frontier social media has revolutionized viral marketing, allowing brands to reach a wider audience and achieve unprecedented levels of engagement. In this chapter, we will explore how AI and frontier social media are impacting influencer marketing, with a focus on the use of AI lenses and filters for selfies, and how these technologies are affecting influencer branding and imaging.

THE RISE OF AI IN VIRAL MARKETING

AI has become an essential tool for viral marketing. With its ability to analyze large amounts of data and identify trends and patterns, AI has made it easier for marketers to create content that resonates with their target audience. AI algorithms can analyze social media activity to identify trending topics, which can then be used to create content that is more likely to go viral. Additionally, AI-powered chatbots can provide personalized customer service, improving customer engagement and increasing the likelihood of viral sharing.

FRONTIER SOCIAL MEDIA AND VIRAL MARKETING

Frontier social media platforms like TikTok and Instagram have become hotbeds for viral marketing campaigns. These platforms are popular among younger audiences, making them ideal for brands targeting younger consumers. The use of influencers on these platforms has been particularly successful, with influencers able to reach millions of followers and create viral content. As a result, influencer marketing has become a key component of many viral marketing campaigns.

One of the most popular forms of content on social media is the selfie, and the use of AI-powered lenses and filters has transformed this simple form of content into a powerful marketing tool. AI-powered lenses and filters can add special effects, animations, and even 3D elements to selfies, making them more engaging and shareable. Brands can use these filters to create branded content, encouraging users to share their branded selfies with their followers.

The Impact on Influencer Branding and Imaging

The use of AI-powered filters and lenses for selfies has also had a significant impact on influencer branding and imaging. Influencers can use these filters to create a consistent image and aesthetic for their brand, making it easier for followers to recognize their content. Additionally, influencers can use these filters to create sponsored content that seamlessly integrates with their personal brand, improving the overall effectiveness of influencer marketing campaigns.

CONCLUSION

Viral marketing has come a long way since the early days of word-of-mouth advertising. The rise of AI and frontier social media has transformed viral marketing into a powerful tool for businesses of all sizes. With the use of AI lenses and filters for selfies, brands can create engaging, shareable content that resonates with their target audience. The impact on influencer branding and imaging has been significant, with influencers able to use these filters to create a consistent image and aesthetic for their personal brand. As AI and frontier social media continue to evolve, viral marketing will remain a vital component of any successful marketing strategy.

Influencer marketing is a type of marketing that involves partnering with individuals with a large following and influence over a specific audience. These individuals, known as influencers, can help brands reach and engage with their target audience through sponsored content or collaborations.

Influencer marketing typically involves identifying influencers who have a significant following on social media platforms such as Instagram, YouTube, or TikTok, and partnering with them to promote a brand, product, or service. Influencers may create sponsored posts or videos featuring the brand or product or collaborate with the brand on a specific campaign or event.

Influencer marketing can be an effective way for brands to reach a wider audience and build credibility with their target market. By partnering with influencers who have already established trust and credibility with their audience, brands can tap into the influencer's influence and reputation to promote their own brand or products.

However, it is important for brands to choose influencers who are a good fit for their brand and target audience, and to ensure that sponsored content is clearly disclosed as such to comply with advertising regulations. Effective influencer marketing requires a strategic approach that aligns with the brand's overall marketing goals and values, and that prioritizes authenticity and transparency in all influencer collaborations.

Influencer marketing has its roots in celebrity endorsements, which have been used in advertising for decades. However, the rise of social media platforms like Instagram, YouTube, and TikTok has led to the emergence of a new kind of influencer: social media influencers who have built large followings and influence through their content.

The first influencer marketing campaigns on social media were relatively simple, involving brands offering free products or payment in exchange for a sponsored post or product review. However, as influencer marketing has grown in popularity, so too has its complexity, with more sophisticated campaigns involving long-term partnerships, event sponsorships, and other creative collaborations.

There are many successful influencer marketers, but some of the most prominent include:

1. Kylie Jenner: Kylie Jenner is a social media influencer and entrepreneur who has leveraged her large following on Instagram and other platforms to promote her own makeup line, Kylie Cosmetics. Her influencer marketing strategy has been highly successful, with her products consistently selling out within minutes of launch.
2. Chiara Ferragni: Chiara Ferragni is an Italian fashion blogger and influencer who has worked with a number of high-end fashion brands, including Dior and Chanel. She has also launched her own fashion line and is widely regarded as one of the most successful influencer marketers in the fashion industry.
3. Zach King: Zach King is a social media influencer and content creator who is known for his creative and engaging videos on platforms like TikTok and Instagram. He has worked with a number of brands, including Coca-Cola and Lego, to create sponsored content that aligns with his unique brand and style.

One of the most infamous influencer marketing campaigns was the Fyre Festival campaign, which was promoted by a number of high-profile influencers on social media. The campaign promised a luxurious, high-end music festival experience on a private island, but ultimately turned out to be a disaster, with attendees left stranded without food or shelter. While the campaign was ultimately a failure, it demonstrates the power of influencer marketing to generate buzz and interest around a brand or event.

Another famous and successful influencer marketing campaigns is the #ShareACoke campaign by Coca-Cola. The campaign involved printing people's names on Coke bottles and cans and encouraging customers to share photos of themselves with their personalized drinks on social media. The campaign was hugely successful, generating over 500,000 photos shared on social media and driving increased sales for Coca-Cola.

Influencer marketing platforms are online marketplaces that connect businesses with influencers who are interested in promoting their products or services. These platforms typically provide a range of tools and services to help businesses identify and connect with influencers, manage influencer campaigns, and track and analyze results. Here's how influencer marketing platforms typically work:

1. Sign Up: Businesses can create an account on the influencer marketing platform and provide information about their brand and campaign goals.
2. Find Influencers: The platform will provide access to a database of influencers who have signed up to be part of the platform. Businesses can search for influencers based on criteria such as niche, audience demographics, and engagement rates.
3. Connect with Influencers: Businesses can send messages or proposals to influencers they are interested in working with, and negotiate the terms of the collaboration.
4. Manage Campaigns: The platform will provide tools for managing influencer campaigns, such as tracking posts and monitoring engagement metrics.
5. Analyze Results: The platform will provide analytics and reporting tools to help businesses measure the effectiveness of their influencer marketing campaigns.

When choosing an influencer marketing platform, businesses should consider factors such as the size and quality of the influencer database, the features and functionality of the platform, the pricing and payment model, and the level of customer support provided.

Some businesses may choose to work with agencies that specialize in influencer marketing to help them identify and connect with influencers, manage campaigns, and analyze results. This can be a good option for businesses that are new to influencer marketing or that need more resources to manage campaigns in-house. However, businesses should carefully evaluate agencies to ensure that they have a track record of success and can provide the services and support they need to achieve their marketing goals.

The main difference between regular influencer marketing and enterprise influencer marketing is the scale and scope of the campaigns.

Regular influencer marketing campaigns typically involve smaller-scale collaborations with individual influencers or small groups of influencers. These campaigns are often focused on raising brand awareness, generating user-generated content, or driving specific actions such as product purchases or social media engagement.

Enterprise influencer marketing, on the other hand, involves larger-scale collaborations with multiple influencers or influencer networks. These campaigns are typically part of broader marketing strategies and may involve various objectives, such as expanding reach, building credibility, or driving sales or leads.

Enterprise influencer marketing campaigns often involve significant investments of time, money, and resources, and require a strategic approach to maximize their impact. They may involve extensive research and analysis to identify the right influencers and platforms, as well as customized content and creative strategies that align with the brand's overall marketing goals and values.

A micro-influencer is an individual who has a smaller but highly engaged social media following, typically ranging from a few thousand to around 100,000 followers. Micro-influencers are often seen as more relatable and trustworthy than larger influencers, as they tend to have a more niche audience and are often seen as experts or authorities in their particular area of interest.

Micro-influencers can be particularly effective for reaching specific audiences and driving engagement and conversions, as their followers tend to be more engaged and invested in their content. Micro-influencer campaigns can also be more cost-effective than larger influencer campaigns, as micro-influencers often charge lower fees and may be more willing to work on a barter or trade basis.

Micro-influencers can be a valuable part of a broader influencer marketing strategy, particularly for brands looking to reach niche audiences or drive engagement and conversions among a specific demographic.

Micro-influencer marketing involves collaborating with individuals who have a smaller but highly engaged social media following, typically ranging from a few thousand to around 100,000 followers. These individuals may specialize in a particular niche, such as food, fashion, beauty, or fitness, and are often seen as experts or authorities in their area of interest.

To launch a micro-influencer campaign, a brand will typically identify relevant micro-influencers based on factors such as their audience demographics, content quality, engagement rates, and overall brand fit. Once identified, the brand will reach out to these micro-influencers to discuss potential collaborations, such as sponsored posts, product reviews, or affiliate partnerships.

Micro-influencer campaigns can be particularly effective for reaching specific audiences and driving engagement and conversions, as micro-influencers tend to have a more niche following and can offer more targeted reach. Micro-influencers also tend to have higher engagement rates than larger influencers, as their followers tend to be more invested and engaged with their content.

Micro-influencer marketing can be a valuable part of a broader influencer marketing strategy, particularly for brands looking to reach niche audiences or drive engagement and conversions among a specific demographic. The key to success in micro-influencer marketing is to identify the right influencers and to collaborate with them in a way that feels authentic and adds value to their followers.

Overall, video marketing has undergone significant changes and transformations over the years, as new technologies and platforms have emerged. However, the ability of video to engage and captivate audiences has remained constant, making it a powerful tool for businesses looking to promote their products and services in the digital age.

Early Days (2000s): The first online video platforms, such as YouTube and Vimeo, were launched in the mid-2000s. Initially, these platforms were primarily used for entertainment and user-generated content, but businesses began to experiment with using video to promote products and services.

The Rise of Viral Videos (2000s): In the mid-2000s, viral videos became a popular way for brands to gain exposure online. These videos were often humorous or unconventional, and relied on social media and word-of-mouth marketing to gain traction. Examples of early viral videos include Blendtec's "Will It Blend?" series and the Old Spice "The Man Your Man Could Smell Like" campaign.

Explainer Videos and Video Ads (2010s): In the early 2010s, businesses began to use video more strategically, creating explainer videos to showcase products and services, and using video ads to promote products on social media and other online platforms. Video ads on platforms such as YouTube and Facebook became increasingly popular, as they allowed brands to target specific audiences and measure the effectiveness of their campaigns.

Live Streaming and Influencer Marketing (2010s-present): In recent years, live streaming has become a popular way for brands to engage with audiences in real-time. Platforms such as Facebook Live and Instagram Live allow businesses to broadcast live events, product launches, and other marketing initiatives to their followers. Additionally, influencer marketing has become a major component of video marketing, with businesses partnering with social media influencers to create brand content and promote products to their followers.

Short-Form Video (2010s-present): The rise of short-form video platforms such as Vine, TikTok, and Instagram Reels has opened new opportunities for businesses to reach younger audiences. These platforms allow users to create and share short, bite-sized videos that are often humorous or creative. Brands have been quick to adopt these platforms, with many creating their own branded content or partnering with popular creators to promote products and services.

Social media provides a unique platform for businesses to reach their target audience, build brand awareness, engage with customers, and ultimately drive sales.

While social media marketing can benefit businesses across various industries, certain types of businesses are particularly well-suited to this type of marketing. These include:

1. E-commerce: Social media provides an excellent platform for promoting e-commerce businesses and driving sales. E-commerce businesses can use social media to showcase their products, run targeted ads, and engage with customers through social media channels.
2. Retail: Retail businesses can use social media to build brand awareness, showcase their products, and drive foot traffic to their physical stores.
3. Hospitality: The hospitality industry can use social media to promote their services, showcase their properties, and engage with customers.
4. Health and wellness: Social media provides an excellent platform for promoting health and wellness businesses, such as gyms, yoga studios, and wellness centers.
5. Entertainment: Social media provides an excellent platform for promoting entertainment businesses, such as movie theaters, music venues, and sports teams.

One famous and successful social media marketing campaign that readers of your book can look up is the "Dilly Dilly" campaign by Bud Light. The campaign was centered around a medieval-themed world and catchphrase called "Dilly Dilly" and was promoted heavily on social media platforms, including Facebook, Twitter, and Instagram.

The "Dilly Dilly" campaign was successful for a number of reasons. Firstly, it was highly engaging and entertaining, capturing the attention of audiences with its humorous and irreverent tone. Secondly, the campaign was highly shareable, with consumers sharing memes, videos, and other content related to the campaign on social media. Lastly, the campaign was highly effective in building brand awareness and loyalty, helping to drive sales and increase market share for Bud Light.

The "Dilly Dilly" campaign by Bud Light worked so well for a few reasons:

1. Creativity: The campaign was highly creative and used a unique medieval theme, which was unlike anything else in the beer industry at the time. The humorous and irreverent tone of the campaign was also highly engaging and entertaining, making it shareable and memorable.
2. Multi-Channel Approach: The campaign was promoted across multiple channels, including television, social media, and in-person activations. This helped to ensure that the campaign reached a wide audience and was able to generate maximum impact.
3. User-Generated Content: The campaign encouraged users to create their own "Dilly Dilly" content and share it on social media, which helped to build a community around the brand and generate buzz.
4. Brand Loyalty: The campaign was effective in building brand loyalty and increasing market share for Bud Light, with consumers becoming more likely to choose Bud Light over competitors.

The "Dilly Dilly" campaign was created by the advertising agency Wieden+Kennedy and was launched in August 2017. The campaign took place over several months and was promoted heavily during major events, such as football games and the Super Bowl.

Bud Light measured the success of the campaign through a range of metrics, including brand awareness, engagement on social media, and sales. The campaign was considered a success, with Bud Light reporting increased sales and market share during the campaign period. Additionally, the "Dilly Dilly" catchphrase became a cultural phenomenon and was widely recognized and shared on social media.

RESOURCES

BOOKS

1. "Reel Marketing: The Video Marketing Guide for Indie Filmmakers and Film Marketers" by James K. Shea
2. "Video Marketing Strategy: Harness the Power of Online Video to Drive Brand Growth" by Jon Mowat
3. "Video Marketing Rules: How to Win in a World Gone Video" by Lou Bortone
4. "The Art of Social Media Video: A Beginner's Guide to Creating Great Video for Facebook, Twitter, Instagram, and More" by Carlos Pacheco
5. "Videocracy: How YouTube Is Changing the World . . . with Double Rainbows, Singing Foxes, and Other Trends We Can't Stop Watching" by Kevin Allocca

WEBSITES

1. Wistia: Wistia is a video hosting and marketing platform that offers a wealth of resources and guides on video marketing, including tips on creating and promoting videos, measuring success, and improving engagement.
2. Vidyard: Vidyard is a video marketing platform that provides resources and tools to help businesses create and optimize video content for marketing and sales purposes. Their website includes a blog with articles and webinars on video marketing best practices.
3. HubSpot: HubSpot is a marketing and sales platform that offers resources and training on a variety of marketing topics, including video marketing. Their website includes a library of free ebooks and guides on video marketing strategy and tactics.
4. Video Brewery: Video Brewery is a video production and marketing agency that provides resources and guides on video marketing best practices, including tips on creating engaging videos and measuring success.
5. Animoto: Animoto is a video creation platform that offers a blog with articles and tutorials on video marketing, as well as a library of free templates and tools for creating videos for social media, advertising, and other purposes.

BeReal marketing is a type of marketing that leverages the BeReal app, a social media app that encourages users to create and share unfiltered, unedited, and authentic content. The app allows users to create short, raw videos that showcase their real lives, rather than the heavily curated and edited content often found on other social media platforms.

BeReal marketing involves using the app to connect with users and build brand awareness in a more authentic and engaging way. Brands can partner with influencers or other users on the app to create branded content that aligns with their values and resonates with their target audience.

One of the key advantages of BeReal marketing is its focus on authenticity and transparency. By using the BeReal app to showcase real, unfiltered moments, brands can build a stronger sense of trust and connection with their audience. BeReal marketing can be particularly effective for brands that are looking to connect with younger, more socially conscious consumers who are looking for more authentic and transparent experiences from the brands they support.

BeReal marketing is a relatively new and emerging form of marketing, but it offers a lot of potential for brands willing to embrace authenticity and transparency as core values in their marketing efforts.

As a relatively new app, there may not be a lot of information available about the most effective BeReal marketing techniques. However, some potential strategies that could be effective include:

1. Influencer marketing: Partnering with social media influencers who align with the values and mission of the BeReal app to promote it to their followers.
2. User-generated content: Encouraging users to share their experiences with the app on social media and using that content to promote the app.
3. Content marketing: Creating and sharing informative, engaging, and relevant content on social media and other channels to attract and educate potential users about the benefits of the BeReal app.
4. Referral programs: Offering incentives or rewards for users who invite their friends to join the app.
5. Community building: Creating a strong community of users who share a common interest in authenticity and vulnerability and who are passionate about spreading the word about the BeReal app.

When dealing with new apps like Bereal, marketers should approach them with an open mind and a willingness to adapt to new platforms and user behaviors. Here are some tips:

1. Keep an eye on emerging trends: Stay up-to-date with new apps and social media platforms that are gaining traction among your target audience.
2. Conduct market research: Understand the platform's user demographics, user behavior, and content consumption habits to develop a marketing strategy that resonates with users.
3. Leverage user-generated content: User-generated content is a powerful way to engage with the app's community and build brand awareness. Consider partnering with micro-influencers or everyday users to create content that is authentic and relatable.
4. Use paid advertising: Consider investing in paid advertising on the app to reach a wider audience and boost your visibility.
5. Test and measure results: Continuously test and measure your marketing campaigns to optimize for the best results. Analyze engagement metrics, click-through rates, and conversion rates to evaluate the effectiveness of your marketing efforts.

One of the most famous success stories of Facebook marketing is the campaign launched by Blendtec for their product, the Blendtec Total Blender. In 2006, the company's CEO Tom Dickson created a series of videos called "Will It Blend?" where he blended various objects, from marbles to iPhones, to showcase the blender's power.

The videos gained a cult following on YouTube, but Blendtec wanted to take it further and reach a wider audience. So they turned to Facebook to promote the campaign, using highly targeted ads and sponsored posts to reach people interested in kitchen appliances and cooking.

The campaign was a huge success, with Blendtec reporting a 700% increase in sales within the first few months of launching the Facebook ads. The company continued to run the campaign for years, creating new "Will It Blend?" videos and using Facebook to promote them.

The success of the campaign is attributed to the highly targeted nature of the Facebook ads, as well as the entertaining and shareable content of the "Will It Blend?" videos. It also demonstrated the power of social media marketing to reach new audiences and drive sales for a product.

Facebook marketing has evolved significantly over the years since the platform's inception in 2004. Here is a brief overview of the major Facebook marketing techniques and systems throughout its history:

1. Early Years (2004-2008): In its early years, Facebook was primarily a social networking site for college students. It was not until 2007 that Facebook opened its platform to advertisers, who could create and place display ads on the site. These ads were relatively simple, consisting of a small image, a headline, and a short description.
2. Facebook Ads (2009-2012): In 2009, Facebook launched its self-serve advertising platform, called Facebook Ads. This allowed advertisers to create and manage their own campaigns, target specific demographics, and track their results. Facebook Ads also introduced the concept of social advertising, which allowed

advertisers to use the personal connections of users to make their ads more relevant and engaging.

3. Open Graph (2012-2015): In 2012, Facebook launched Open Graph, which enabled third-party apps and websites to integrate with Facebook. This allowed for more targeted and personalized advertising, as Facebook could use data from these integrations to better understand users and their interests. Open Graph also introduced the concept of social plugins, which allowed websites to display Facebook content, such as Like buttons and comments, on their pages.

4. Facebook Marketing Partners (2015-Present): In 2015, Facebook launched its Marketing Partners program, which provided a directory of companies that specialized in various aspects of Facebook marketing, such as ad creation and optimization, data management, and audience targeting. The program also included a certification process to ensure that partners met Facebook's standards for quality and expertise.

5. Facebook Pixel (2015-Present): In 2015, Facebook introduced the Facebook Pixel, which is a piece of code that can be added to a website to track user behavior and activity. The Pixel allows advertisers to retarget users who have visited their website, create custom audiences based on specific actions, and measure the effectiveness of their campaigns.

6. Messenger Ads (2016-Present): In 2016, Facebook introduced Messenger Ads, which allowed advertisers to place ads within the Messenger app. These ads appeared between conversations and could be used to promote products or services, or to start a conversation with a potential customer.

Facebook marketing offers several advantages over other types of social media marketing, including a large audience, advanced targeting options, comprehensive analytics, and a variety of ad formats. Facebook also provides robust ad management tools, making it easier for businesses to create and manage ad campaigns. Additionally, Facebook tends to have high levels of engagement, which can help brands build a stronger connection with their audience.

Table 3 - Facebook Marketing Advantages

	Facebook Marketing	Other Social Media Marketing
Advantages		
Large audience	✔☐	✔☐
Advanced targeting	✔☐	✔☐
Comprehensive analytics	✔☐	✔☐
Variety of ad formats	✔☐	✔☐
Robust ad management tools	✔☐	✔☐
High engagement levels	✔☐	Depends on the platform
Disadvantages		
High competition	☐	Depends on the platform
Can be expensive	☐	Depends on the platform
Algorithm changes can impact reach	☐	Depends on the platform
Ad fatigue	☐	Depends on the platform

Facebook marketing can indeed seem complex, but here is a simplified breakdown of the various segments and categories within Facebook marketing:

1. Organic Marketing: This involves creating and sharing content on your Facebook page without paying for ads. Organic marketing is all about engaging with your audience and building a community around your brand.
2. Paid Advertising: This involves creating and running ads on Facebook to reach a wider audience and drive traffic or conversions. Facebook offers a range of ad formats, including image ads, video ads, carousel ads, and more. Ad targeting options include demographic targeting, interests targeting, lookalike audiences, and retargeting.
3. Facebook Pixel: The Facebook pixel is a piece of code that you place on your website to track user behavior and gather data about your website visitors. The pixel can be used to create custom audiences for your Facebook ads, track conversions, and optimize your ad campaigns.

4. Insights and Analytics: Facebook offers a range of insights and analytics tools that businesses can use to measure the effectiveness of their Facebook marketing efforts. These tools allow businesses to track metrics like reach, engagement, click-through rates, and conversions, and adjust their strategy based on these insights.

In terms of how Facebook marketing works, it's important to note that it's not just about buying and managing ads. Successful Facebook marketing involves creating a cohesive strategy that leverages both organic and paid marketing tactics and uses data and insights to continually refine and optimize your approach.

One important element of successful Facebook marketing is understanding how the Facebook algorithm works and using that knowledge to your advantage. The algorithm is designed to show users content that is relevant and engaging, so businesses that create content that is highly shareable and engaging are more likely to see success on the platform.

Facebook marketing can be a highly effective way for businesses to reach and engage with their target audience, drive traffic and sales, and build a strong online presence. By leveraging a range of organic and paid marketing tactics, and using data and insights to guide your strategy, businesses can achieve great success on the platform.

One factor that sets Instagram marketing apart from other social media marketing is its focus on visual content. Instagram is primarily a platform for sharing photos and videos, which makes it a popular platform for businesses in visually-driven industries like fashion, beauty, and travel. Instagram's visual nature also allows businesses to showcase their products and services in a creative and engaging way, which can help to build brand awareness and loyalty.

Another advantage of Instagram marketing is its large and active user base. Instagram currently has over 1 billion monthly active users, and users on the platform are highly engaged with content. This can make it an effective platform for businesses looking to build a following and engage with their audience.

However, the relationship with its parent company, Meta (formerly Facebook), could potentially impact Instagram's marketing potential. In recent years, Meta has faced scrutiny over privacy concerns and data breaches, which could impact user trust in the platform. Additionally, changes to Meta's advertising policies could impact Instagram's advertising capabilities and potentially limit the reach of businesses on the platform.

Despite these potential challenges, Instagram marketing remains a valuable tool for businesses looking to reach a younger, more visually-focused audience. By leveraging the platform's visual nature and engaging with its active user base, businesses can build brand awareness and connect with their target audience on a deeper level.

LinkedIn marketing involves promoting a brand or business on the LinkedIn platform to connect with a professional audience. As the world's largest professional network, LinkedIn has over 740 million members in more than 200 countries, making it a valuable platform for businesses looking to reach a professional audience.

LinkedIn marketing works by creating and sharing content on the platform, including company updates, articles, and sponsored content. Brands can also use LinkedIn's advertising tools to reach a targeted audience, including sponsored content, sponsored InMail, and display ads.

One advantage of LinkedIn marketing is its highly targeted audience. LinkedIn users are professionals who are interested in networking, career development, and industry news. This makes it an ideal platform for B2B marketers and businesses looking to reach a professional audience.

LinkedIn also offers a number of features that can help businesses engage with their audience, including LinkedIn Groups, which allow professionals to connect and discuss industry topics, and LinkedIn Pulse, a publishing platform that allows businesses to share thought leadership content with a wider audience.

LinkedIn marketing can be an effective way to reach a professional audience and build brand awareness. However, as with any marketing strategy, it's important to consider your target audience and marketing goals before investing in LinkedIn marketing.

Figure 2 - Snapchat Marketing Quotes

Quote	Author
"Snapchat is where the <u>under-35 crowd</u> lives. If that's your target audience, then you need to be on Snapchat."	Forbes magazine
"<u>Snapchat</u> is a reflection of how people communicate with each other in real life."	<u>Neil Patel</u>, digital marketing expert
"Snapchat is a platform that demands creativity. Brands that think outside the box and take risks will be rewarded."	Entrepreneur magazine
"Snapchat is the go-to platform for reaching the elusive Gen Z audience."	Adweek

Snapchat marketing can be an effective way to reach a younger, more engaged audience, particularly among millennials and Generation Z. While Snapchat's user base may be a narrower niche than other social media platforms like Facebook or Instagram, it still boasts over 280 million daily active users.

Snapchat marketing works by creating and sharing content on the platform, including snaps (photos or videos up to 60 seconds in length), stories (compilations of snaps that last 24 hours), and lenses or filters that can be used to augment snaps. Businesses can create sponsored lenses or filters, run sponsored ads, or partner with influencers on the platform to reach their target audience.

One advantage of Snapchat marketing is the high engagement levels of its users. Snapchat users spend an average of 30 minutes per day on the platform and are more likely to interact with branded content than users on other platforms. Additionally, Snapchat offers unique features like augmented reality lenses and geofilters that can enhance the user experience and increase engagement with branded content.

However, as with any marketing strategy, it's important for businesses to consider their target audience and marketing goals before deciding to invest in Snapchat marketing. If your target audience does not align with Snapchat's user base or your marketing goals do not align with the platform's capabilities, it may not be the best fit for your business. Additionally, Snapchat marketing may require a more creative and engaging approach than other platforms, which can be a challenge for some businesses.

Twitter marketing is a form of social media marketing that involves using the Twitter platform to promote a brand, product, or service. Twitter is a popular social media platform that allows users to share short, concise messages called tweets with their followers. Businesses can leverage Twitter to build brand awareness, engage with customers, and drive traffic and sales.

Some common tactics used in Twitter marketing include:

1. Creating and sharing content that is relevant and valuable to your target audience.
2. Engaging with followers and participating in conversations related to your industry or niche.
3. Using Twitter ads to reach a wider audience and promote specific products or services.
4. Monitoring mentions and hashtags related to your brand or industry and responding to feedback or inquiries in a timely manner.
5. Collaborating with influencers or other brands to amplify your reach and increase engagement.

Twitter also offers a range of analytics tools that businesses can use to measure the effectiveness of their Twitter marketing efforts. These tools allow businesses to track metrics like engagement rates, follower growth, and click-through rates, and make adjustments to their strategy based on these insights.

Twitter marketing can be an effective way for businesses to build brand awareness, engage with customers, and drive traffic and sales, particularly for brands that have a strong social media presence and a highly engaged audience.

YouTube marketing refers to the practice of using the YouTube platform to promote a brand, product, or service. It involves creating and publishing videos on YouTube that are designed to engage viewers, build brand awareness, and drive traffic and sales. YouTube marketing can take many forms, from educational videos to product demonstrations to influencer collaborations.

Here's a brief overview of how YouTube marketing works:

1. Create and publish videos: The first step in YouTube marketing is to create and publish videos that are relevant and engaging to your target audience. This may involve conducting research to identify the types of videos that resonate with your audience, and creating content that addresses their needs and interests.
2. Optimize for search: YouTube is a search engine, and optimizing your videos for search can help ensure that they are discoverable by your target audience. This may involve using relevant keywords in your video titles and descriptions, as well as adding tags and annotations to help users find your content.
3. Promote your videos: Once you've published your videos on YouTube, it's important to promote them through various channels such as social media, email, and your website. This can help drive traffic to your videos and increase engagement and views.
4. Measure and analyze results: To measure the effectiveness of your YouTube marketing efforts, it's important to track key metrics such as views, engagement, and conversions. This can help you identify areas for improvement and optimize your future videos and campaigns.

Some famous and prominent figures in YouTube marketing include:

1. PewDiePie: Felix Kjellberg, known as PewDiePie, is a popular YouTube personality who has amassed over 110 million subscribers on his channel. He is known for his gaming content and has also collaborated with brands on sponsored content.
2. Zoella: Zoe Sugg, known as Zoella, is a British YouTuber who has gained a large following for her beauty and lifestyle content. She

has also collaborated with brands on sponsored content and has released her own beauty products.

3. Casey Neistat: Casey Neistat is a filmmaker and YouTuber who has gained a large following for his vlogs and video essays. He has also worked with brands on sponsored content and has collaborated with other YouTubers on various projects.

4. Michelle Phan: Michelle Phan is a beauty YouTuber who has gained a large following for her makeup tutorials and beauty advice. She has also collaborated with brands on sponsored content and has launched her own makeup line.

These figures have been successful in building a large following on YouTube and using their platform to promote themselves and their brands. While their strategies and approaches may differ, they all share a commitment to creating high-quality, engaging content that resonates with their audience.

TIKTOK MARKETING

YouTube marketing, TikTok marketing, and social media marketing all have unique characteristics and approaches. Here are some of the key differences between the three:

VIDEO LENGTH

TikTok marketing is the practice of using the TikTok platform to promote a brand, product, or service. TikTok is a video-based social media platform that allows users to create and share short-form videos, typically between 15 and 60 seconds in length. Here are some key aspects of TikTok marketing:

Advantages of TikTok's Video Length:

1. Attention-Grabbing: TikTok videos are short and designed to capture attention quickly. This makes them ideal for engaging younger audiences and holding their attention for the duration of the video.
2. Shareability: Short videos are more easily shareable than longer ones. TikTok videos can be shared directly within the app, making it easy for users to share with friends and family.
3. Quick to Produce: Short videos can be produced quickly and easily. This makes it easier for brands to create and publish videos on a regular basis, without the need for extensive production resources.

Disadvantages of TikTok's Video Length:

1. Limited Time to Convey Information: With such a short video length, it can be challenging to convey a lot of information or tell a complete story. Marketers must find creative ways to convey their message within the limited time frame.
2. Short Attention Span: While TikTok videos are designed to capture attention quickly, they can also lose viewers' attention just as quickly. Marketers must ensure that their videos are engaging from start to finish to avoid losing viewers.

Leveraging TikTok's Video Length:

1. Use Short-Form Storytelling: TikTok videos can tell a story or convey a message in just a few seconds. Marketers can leverage this by using short-form storytelling to create engaging and memorable videos.
2. Be Creative: With limited time to convey information, marketers must find creative ways to capture their audience's attention and convey their message. This can involve using humor, music, or other creative elements to make their videos stand out.
3. Use Influencers: TikTok influencers can be a valuable asset for brands looking to reach a wider audience. Influencers can create branded content that aligns with the brand's message and values.

Uncommon Applications of TikTok's Video Length:

1. Product Teasers: Short videos can be used to tease new products or features, building anticipation and excitement among users.
2. Behind-the-Scenes Content: Short videos can offer a behind-the-scenes look at a brand's products or services, providing users with a unique and authentic perspective.
3. Interactive Content: Short videos can be used to create interactive content, such as quizzes or polls, that engage users and encourage participation.

Famous Examples of TikTok Marketing:

1. Chipotle: Chipotle launched a TikTok campaign called #GuacDance, in which users could create and share videos of themselves doing the "guac dance" for a chance to win free chips and guacamole.
2. Elf Cosmetics: Elf Cosmetics partnered with TikTok influencers to create a viral dance challenge called the #eyeslipsface challenge, which generated over 4 billion views on the platform.
3. Ocean Spray: A video of a TikTok user riding a skateboard and drinking Ocean Spray cranberry juice went viral, prompting the brand to partner with the user and create a sponsored video that garnered over 11 million views.

Audience Demographics

Another difference between the three is the audience demographics. YouTube has a broad audience, with a large number of users across different age groups and interests. TikTok, on the other hand, is popular among younger audiences, with a significant portion of users under the age of 30. Social media marketing, in general, can vary depending on the platform and the audience demographics.

Content Strategy

Each platform has its own unique content strategy. YouTube is ideal for longer-form content, such as tutorials and product demonstrations, while TikTok is better suited for short-form videos that are highly engaging and visually compelling. Social media marketing involves a variety of content types, from text posts to images and videos, and requires a more diverse content strategy.

Influencer Marketing

Influencer marketing is an important component of marketing on all three platforms, but the approach can differ. On YouTube, brands often partner with influencers for sponsored content and collaborations. On TikTok, influencers are often the content creators themselves, and brands may partner with them for product placements or branded content. Social media marketing can involve both approaches, depending on the platform and the audience.

Metrics and Analytics

The metrics and analytics for each platform differ as well. YouTube and TikTok have their own analytics tools to track views, engagement, and other metrics. Social media platforms also offer their own analytics tools, but the data can be more fragmented across different platforms.

YouTube marketing, TikTok marketing, and social media marketing each have their own unique characteristics and approaches. Understanding the differences between the three can help businesses develop an effective marketing strategy that targets the right audience and delivers the right message on the right platform.

Before the internet, advertising platforms were mostly traditional media such as television, radio, newspapers, and billboards. These mediums allowed businesses to reach a large audience with their message, but the targeting options were limited, and the reach was not as precise as it is with digital advertising platforms.

Television advertising was a popular advertising platform before the internet, with businesses buying airtime during popular shows to reach a broad audience. Radio advertising was also common, with businesses creating catchy jingles and commercials to promote their products or services. Newspapers were another popular advertising platform, with businesses placing ads in print newspapers to reach local audiences. Outdoor advertising, such as billboards and signs, was also common, especially for local businesses looking to reach drivers and pedestrians in a specific area.

Before the internet, there was also direct mail marketing, where businesses would send promotional material directly to customers' mailboxes. This form of advertising was often used for targeted marketing campaigns, such as sending catalogs or brochures to specific demographics.

Advertising platforms before the internet were less sophisticated than they are today, with limited targeting options and less precise measurement of results. However, they were still effective in reaching broad audiences and building brand awareness for businesses.

Advertising platforms are digital platforms that enable businesses to promote their products or services to a specific audience through various forms of online advertising. Almost all of the most popular social media platforms have advertising platforms that businesses can use to reach their target audiences. Social media platforms such as Facebook, Instagram, Twitter, and LinkedIn have robust advertising platforms that allow businesses to create and run ads to specific audiences based on demographics, interests, behaviors, and more. These platforms offer a variety of ad formats and targeting options, making it easier for businesses to reach their desired audience with the right message at the right time.

Some examples of advertising platforms include:

1. Google Ads
2. Facebook Ads
3. Instagram Ads
4. Twitter Ads
5. LinkedIn Ads
6. Amazon Advertising
7. YouTube Ads
8. TikTok Ads
9. Snapchat Ads

Google Ads (formerly known as Google AdWords) was launched in October 2000, two years after the launch of Google's search engine. When Google first launched, it was a simple search engine that returned text-based results based on user queries.

In the early days of Google, the company did not have a clear revenue model, and advertising was not a priority. However, as the company grew, it became clear that advertising could be a significant source of revenue. In 1999, Google launched its first advertising program, which was called "Google Sponsorships." The program allowed businesses to pay a flat fee to be listed at the top of search results for specific keywords.

In 2000, Google launched AdWords, which allowed businesses to create and run text-based ads that would appear on Google search results pages. Advertisers could bid on keywords and pay per click on their ads. The AdWords platform was initially very basic, with limited targeting options and no conversion tracking. However, it was an instant success, and many businesses began using it to drive traffic to their websites.

Over the next few years, Google continued to develop the AdWords platform, adding new features such as location targeting, ad scheduling, and conversion tracking. In 2003, Google introduced the AdSense program, which allowed website owners to display AdWords ads on their sites and earn a portion of the revenue generated from clicks.

By 2004, Google Ads had become a major source of revenue for the company, and it continued to grow in popularity as more businesses began using it. Over the years, Google has continued to add new features and capabilities to the platform, making it one of the most influential and sophisticated advertising platforms available today.

Google Ads is one of the most popular advertising platform. It allows businesses to create ads that appear on Google search results pages and other Google properties such as YouTube, Google Maps, and partner websites.

Amazon Advertising, formerly known as Amazon Marketing Services, was launched in 2012, more than 15 years after the launch of the Amazon store. When Amazon first launched in 1994, it was a simple online bookstore that sold books to customers over the internet.

In the early years of Amazon, advertising was not a major focus for the company. Instead, Amazon primarily focused on building a user-friendly online store and expanding its product offerings beyond books.

It wasn't until 2003 that Amazon introduced its first advertising product, called Amazon Text Ads. The program allowed businesses to create and display text-based ads on Amazon.com and pay on a cost-per-click basis. However, the program was short-lived and was discontinued in 2008.

In 2006, Amazon introduced its second advertising product, called Amazon Product Ads. The program allowed businesses to display product ads on Amazon.com and pay on a cost-per-click basis. However, the program was limited in scope and was only available to businesses that had their own e-commerce websites.

It wasn't until 2012 that Amazon Advertising as we know it today was launched. The program allowed businesses to create and display ads on Amazon.com and the Amazon network of websites and devices, including Kindle e-readers, Fire tablets, and Fire TV. Amazon Advertising initially offered limited targeting options, but over time, the platform has added more advanced targeting options and features.

Amazon Advertising is a major source of revenue for Amazon and is one of the most popular advertising platforms available to businesses. It allows businesses to reach millions of Amazon customers with highly targeted ads based on their search and purchase behavior.

Microsoft Advertising (formerly known as Bing Ads) is a pay-per-click advertising platform that allows businesses to display ads on the Microsoft Search Network, which includes Bing, Yahoo, and AOL search engines. Microsoft Advertising works similarly to other pay-per-click platforms, such as Google Ads, where businesses bid on keywords and pay per click on their ads.

Microsoft Advertising offers a variety of targeting options, including location targeting, device targeting, and audience targeting based on demographics, interests, and behaviors. The platform also offers conversion tracking and optimization tools to help businesses track and improve their ad performance.

Microsoft Advertising may not have the same level of reach as Google Ads, but it can still be a worthwhile advertising platform for businesses, particularly those targeting specific demographics or industries. Microsoft Search Network users tend to be older and have higher incomes, making it a good platform for businesses targeting older audiences or those in more specialized industries.

In addition, Microsoft Advertising often has lower competition than Google Ads, which can result in lower cost-per-clicks and a higher return on investment for businesses.

Whether or not Microsoft Advertising is worth considering for your business will depend on your target audience and advertising goals. It's always a good idea to test different advertising platforms and see which ones work best for your business.

Traditional digital marketing has undergone significant changes and transformations over the years, as new technologies and platforms have emerged. However, many of the core principles of marketing such as understanding your target audience, providing value, building relationships, and measuring results have remained consistent.

Early Days (1990s-2000s): The early days of digital marketing were characterized by the rise of the internet and the World Wide Web. During this time, businesses began to experiment with online advertising in the form of banner ads and pop-ups. However, these ads were often seen as intrusive and annoying, and many consumers began to use ad-blocking software to avoid them.

Search Engine Marketing (2000s): In the early 2000s, search engines such as Google and Yahoo! began to offer pay-per-click (PPC) advertising, which allowed businesses to bid on keywords and place ads in search engine results pages (SERPs). This marked the beginning of search engine marketing (SEM), which has since become a major component of digital marketing.

Social Media Marketing (2000s-2010s): The rise of social media platforms such as Facebook, Twitter, and LinkedIn in the late 2000s and early 2010s opened up new opportunities for digital marketers. Brands began to use social media to engage with customers, build relationships, and promote products and services. Social media marketing has since become a major component of digital marketing, with platforms such as Instagram and TikTok offering new opportunities for brands to reach their target audience.

Content Marketing (2010s): As consumers became more skeptical of traditional advertising, brands began to focus more on content marketing, which involves creating and sharing valuable, relevant, and consistent content to attract and retain a clearly defined audience. Content marketing has become an essential part of digital marketing, with brands using a variety of channels such as blogs, videos, and social media to engage with their target audience.

Mobile Marketing (2010s-present): The rise of smartphones and mobile devices has opened up new opportunities for digital marketers to reach consumers on-the-go. Mobile marketing includes tactics such as SMS marketing, mobile apps, and mobile advertising, which are specifically designed to target consumers on their mobile devices.

Artificial Intelligence and Machine Learning (2010s-present): With the rise of artificial intelligence (AI) and machine learning, digital marketers have new tools at their disposal to analyze data, optimize campaigns, and improve customer targeting. AI-powered chatbots, for example, can provide instant customer service and support, while machine learning algorithms can analyze vast amounts of data to identify patterns and insights that would be difficult or impossible for humans to detect.

DIGITAL MARKETING KPIs

Digital marketing KPIs (Key Performance Indicators) are measurable values that help marketers track the success of their digital marketing campaigns. KPIs can be used to measure a range of different metrics, including website traffic, social media engagement, email open rates, conversion rates, and more.

While some digital marketing KPIs may be universal across different genres of digital marketing, such as website traffic and conversion rates, others may be more specific to certain types of marketing. For example, engagement metrics, such as likes, comments, and shares, are more relevant to social media marketing, while view counts and watch time may be more relevant to video marketing.

In general, it's important for marketers to identify the KPIs that are most relevant to their specific marketing goals and strategies. For example, if the goal of a social media marketing campaign is to increase brand awareness, metrics such as reach and impressions may be more important, while if the goal is to drive sales, metrics such as click-through rates and conversion rates may be more important.

Ultimately, while some digital marketing KPIs may be similar across different genres of digital marketing, it's important for marketers to identify the specific KPIs that are most relevant to their goals and strategies in order to effectively measure and track the success of their campaigns.

Table 1 - Abbreviated Table of Digital Marketing KPIs

Marketing Category	KPI	Quantification	Evaluation
Social Media Marketing	Reach	The number of unique people who saw your content	Higher reach indicates that more people have been exposed to your content
Social Media Marketing	Engagement Rate	The percentage of people who engaged with your content (e.g. likes, comments, shares) compared to the number of people who saw it	Higher engagement rate indicates that your content is resonating with your audience and generating more interactions
Social Media Marketing	Click-Through Rate (CTR)	The percentage of people who clicked on a link in your content compared to the number of people who saw it	Higher CTR indicates that your content is compelling and driving more traffic to your website or landing page
Email Marketing	Open Rate	The percentage of people who opened your email	Higher open rate indicates that your subject line and email content is compelling and relevant to your audience
Email Marketing	Click-Through Rate (CTR)	The percentage of people who clicked on a link in your email compared to the number of people who opened it	Higher CTR indicates that your email content is compelling and driving more traffic to your website or landing page
Content Marketing	Pageviews	The number of times a page on your website has been viewed	Higher pageviews indicate that your content is driving traffic to your website
Content Marketing	Time on Page	The amount of time visitors spend on a page on your website	Higher time on page indicates that your content is engaging and keeping visitors interested
Content Marketing	Bounce Rate	The percentage of visitors who leave your website after only viewing one page	Lower bounce rate indicates that visitors are finding your content relevant and engaging enough to explore your website further

One famous case study related to digital marketing KPIs is the "Old Spice" campaign by Procter & Gamble. The campaign, which ran from 2010 to 2012, was centered around a series of humorous and irreverent commercials that featured the actor Isaiah Mustafa.

One of the key KPIs that the Old Spice campaign focused on was social media engagement. The campaign was highly successful in this regard, generating over 1.4 billion impressions and 8 million views on YouTube. In addition, the campaign resulted in a 107% increase in Old Spice body wash sales in the year following the campaign.

To measure social media engagement, the Old Spice campaign focused on a range of KPIs, including likes, comments, shares, and follower growth. These metrics were used to track the success of the campaign across various social media platforms, including Facebook, Twitter, and YouTube.

One notable example of the success of the Old Spice campaign was the "Responses" campaign, in which Old Spice created and uploaded 186 personalized video responses to fans on YouTube and other social media platforms. This campaign generated over 40 million views and 180,000 comments, driving increased engagement and brand loyalty.

The Old Spice campaign is a great example of how effective digital marketing KPIs can be in measuring the success of a campaign. By focusing on social media engagement and other relevant KPIs, Old Spice was able to track the success of their campaign and generate significant business results.

PPC (Pay-Per-Click) marketing is a type of digital marketing in which advertisers pay a fee each time one of their ads is clicked on. This model is often used in search engine advertising, where advertisers bid on keywords related to their products or services, and their ads are displayed to users who search for those keywords.

PPC marketing is still very relevant today and is used by a wide range of businesses, including e-commerce companies, local businesses, and B2B organizations. PPC advertising can be an effective way to drive traffic and conversions, especially for businesses that are just starting out and need to quickly generate leads or sales.

One of the main advantages of PPC advertising is that it allows businesses to target specific audiences based on factors such as location, interests, and demographics. This can help to ensure that ads are shown to people who are most likely to be interested in a business's products or services, which can increase the likelihood of conversions.

Overall, while there are many different types of digital marketing strategies, PPC advertising remains a popular and effective option for businesses of all sizes and industries.

SEO (Search Engine Optimization) marketing is still very relevant, even with the rise of AI and NLP engines. In fact, AI and NLP engines can actually make SEO even more important, as they rely on the same principles as traditional search engines when it comes to indexing and ranking web pages.

SEO is the practice of optimizing a website to improve its visibility and ranking in search engine results pages (SERPs). While the algorithms used by search engines are constantly evolving, the basic principles of SEO remain the same: creating high-quality content, optimizing on-page elements (such as meta tags and headers), building high-quality backlinks, and using relevant keywords.

While AI and NLP engines may be changing the way people search for information, they are still reliant on the same basic principles of SEO. Search engines and AI-powered search platforms rely on relevant, high-quality content that is optimized for the keywords and topics being searched for. By using SEO best practices, businesses can ensure that their content is easily discoverable and accessible to users, regardless of the search platform they are using.

While the landscape of search engines and search technologies may be evolving, SEO remains an important and effective digital marketing strategy for businesses of all sizes and industries.

DISPLAY MARKETING

Display marketing, also known as display advertising, is a form of online advertising that involves placing banner ads, videos, and other forms of visual content on third-party websites. Display ads are typically placed on websites that are relevant to the advertiser's target audience and are designed to generate interest in the advertiser's products or services.

BOOKS

The following reading list contains some of the best and most recommended books on digital marketing. The list covers various topics ranging from Google AdWords, SEO, landing page optimization, web analytics, copywriting, conversion optimization, display advertising, and more. These books provide valuable insights and practical tips that help marketers understand the complex world of digital marketing and improve their online results. Whether you are a beginner or an experienced marketer, these books are a must-read to stay up-to-date with the latest trends and strategies in the field of digital marketing.

1. "Advanced Google AdWords" by Brad Geddes
2. "The Ultimate Guide to Google AdWords" by Perry Marshall, Mike Rhodes, and Bryan Todd
3. "The Art of SEO" by Eric Enge, Stephan Spencer, and Jessie Stricchiola
4. "Web Analytics 2.0" by Avinash Kaushik
5. "Landing Page Optimization" by Tim Ash, Maura Ginty, and Rich Page
6. "The New Rules of Marketing and PR" by David Meerman Scott
7. "The Adweek Copywriting Handbook" by Joseph Sugarman
8. "Conversion Optimization: The Art and Science of Converting Prospects into Customers" by Khalid Saleh and Ayat Shukairy
9. "Call to Action: Secret Formulas to Improve Online Results" by Bryan Eisenberg, Jeffrey Eisenberg, and Lisa T. Davis
10. "Display Advertising: An Hour a Day" by David Booth and Corey Koberg.

One famous and successful display marketing campaign is Nike's "Just Do It" campaign. The campaign, which launched in 1988, aimed to position Nike as a brand that inspired and motivated people to be active and pursue their goals.

The campaign included a range of different marketing tactics, including print ads, television commercials, and display ads. One notable display ad featured a photo of a runner on a misty road with the tagline "Just Do It" superimposed over the image. The ad was designed to evoke a sense of determination and motivation, and it quickly became an iconic part of the campaign.

The "Just Do It" campaign was a huge success for Nike, helping to increase the brand's market share and establish Nike as a leader in the athletic apparel industry. The campaign's use of display advertising, along with other marketing tactics, helped to build brand awareness and drive sales for Nike.

The "Just Do It" campaign is a great example of how display marketing can be used to build brand awareness and drive sales for a business. By placing ads on relevant third-party websites and using compelling visual content, businesses can reach their target audience and generate interest in their products or services.

Email marketing can be very profitable for businesses when executed effectively. According to a recent study by the DMA (Direct Marketing Association), email marketing has an average ROI of $42 for every $1 spent, making it one of the most cost-effective marketing channels available.

One famous and successful email marketing campaign is the Obama campaign's email fundraising campaign during the 2012 US presidential election. The campaign used a combination of email marketing and social media marketing to mobilize supporters and raise funds for the campaign.

The campaign's email marketing efforts were particularly successful, with the campaign sending out regular updates and fundraising requests to its email list. The campaign's emails were personalized, engaging, and focused on motivating supporters to act and donate to the campaign.

One key reason for the success of the Obama campaign's email marketing efforts was its use of data analytics and segmentation. The campaign used data analytics to track the behavior and preferences of its email subscribers, allowing them to segment their list and send targeted messages to specific groups of supporters.

Another important factor in the campaign's success was its use of storytelling and emotional appeals. The campaign's emails often featured stories of individual supporters who had been helped by Obama's policies or who had been inspired by his leadership, creating an emotional connection with readers and motivating them to take action.

While email may not be the preferred communication channel for certain demographics, it remains a highly effective marketing channel for many businesses. By using personalization, segmentation, and compelling content, businesses can use email marketing to build relationships with their subscribers, drive traffic and sales, and achieve a strong ROI.

Related Books

1. "The Audacity to Win: The Inside Story and Lessons of Barack Obama's Historic Victory" by David Plouffe
2. "Yes We Did! An Inside Look at How Social Media Built the Obama Brand" by Rahaf Harfoush
3. "The Victory Lab: The Secret Science of Winning Campaigns" by Sasha Issenberg
4. "The Obama Syndrome: Surrender at Home, War Abroad" by Tariq Ali (discusses the Obama campaign's use of marketing tactics)

Say what you will about Obama's politics, one of the main reasons why he was able to eke out a second term was largely due to his email marketing campaign. The Obama campaign's email marketing campaign during the 2012 US presidential election was designed and executed by the campaign's in-house digital team, led by Director of

Digital Strategy, Teddy Goff. The team included designers, developers, writers, and data analysts, who worked together to create a highly effective email marketing campaign that helped to mobilize supporters and raise funds for the campaign.

One of the key technologies used by the Obama campaign's email marketing team was data analytics. The team used a combination of data analytics tools, including Blue State Digital's proprietary platform, to track the behavior and preferences of their email subscribers. This allowed the team to segment their list and send targeted messages to specific groups of supporters based on their interests, demographics, and past behavior.

Another important technology used by the Obama campaign's email marketing team was responsive design. The team recognized early on that a significant percentage of their email subscribers were accessing their emails on mobile devices, so they prioritized designing emails that were optimized for mobile viewing. This involved using responsive design techniques to ensure that emails would render properly on screens of all sizes and resolutions.

In terms of the campaign's email design and architecture, the team used a range of techniques to make their emails engaging and effective. This included using attention-grabbing subject lines, personalized greetings, and compelling visuals to capture readers' attention and motivate them to take action. The team also made strategic use of storytelling and emotional appeals to create a sense of connection and urgency among readers.

The success of the Obama campaign's email marketing campaign can be attributed to a combination of factors, including the use of data analytics and segmentation, responsive design, and compelling content. While the campaign's email marketing efforts were groundbreaking in their use of these techniques, many of the best practices they employed are still highly effective in email marketing today.

E-commerce platforms are considered marketing platforms because they provide businesses with a way to reach a wider audience and promote their products or services to potential customers. E-commerce platforms allow businesses to create an online storefront, list their products, and reach a global audience. By providing businesses with tools to showcase their products and make transactions online, e-commerce platforms can be an effective marketing tool for businesses of all sizes. Some examples of e-commerce platforms that also function as marketing platforms include:

1. Shopify: Shopify is an e-commerce platform that allows businesses to create an online store, manage inventory, and process payments. Shopify also offers a variety of marketing tools, including email marketing, social media integrations, and SEO optimization.
2. WooCommerce: WooCommerce is a plugin for WordPress that allows businesses to turn their website into an e-commerce store. WooCommerce offers a variety of marketing features, including email marketing, social media integrations, and affiliate marketing tools.
3. Magento: Magento is an open-source e-commerce platform that offers businesses a customizable storefront, payment processing, and order management tools. Magento also offers a variety of marketing features, including SEO optimization, email marketing, and social media integrations.
4. Amazon: Amazon is the world's largest online marketplace, and it offers businesses a way to list their products and reach a global audience. Amazon also offers a variety of marketing features, including advertising options, email marketing, and customer reviews.

E-commerce platforms are considered marketing platforms because they provide businesses with a way to reach a wider audience, promote their products or services, and increase sales. By offering a range of marketing tools and integrations, e-commerce platforms can be an effective tool for businesses looking to expand their online presence and grow their customer base.

Customer review platforms are online platforms where customers can leave reviews and feedback about businesses, products, or services they have used. These platforms allow customers to share their experiences and opinions with others and help businesses build their reputation and improve their products or services. Marketers can use customer review platforms in a number of ways, including:

1. Reputation management: Marketers can monitor customer reviews to track their company's online reputation and respond to negative feedback in a timely and effective manner.
2. Customer feedback: Marketers can use customer reviews to gain insights into customer preferences, pain points, and areas for improvement. This feedback can be used to refine products, services, and marketing strategies.
3. Social proof: Positive customer reviews can serve as social proof, helping to build trust with potential customers and encourage them to make a purchase.

One successful case study of a customer review platform is TripAdvisor. TripAdvisor is a travel review platform where customers can leave reviews and feedback about hotels, restaurants, and other travel-related businesses. The platform has more than 830 million reviews and opinions and is one of the most popular travel review platforms in the world.

TripAdvisor has been successful because it has leveraged the power of customer reviews to build trust with potential travelers. The platform uses a variety of tools and features, such as traveler rankings, traveler photos, and the ability to filter reviews by traveler type and date of stay, to help users find the most relevant and useful information.

Businesses listed on TripAdvisor can also use the platform to promote their products and services, respond to customer feedback, and monitor their online reputation. By using TripAdvisor, businesses can leverage the power of customer reviews to build trust with potential customers and increase bookings and revenue.

Deep linking marketing is a technique that allows marketers to link directly to a specific page or feature within an app, rather than just the app's homepage. This technique can be useful for driving user engagement and improving the user experience by making it easier for users to access specific content within an app.

The concept of deep linking dates back to the early days of the internet, when hypertext links were first introduced. However, it wasn't until the rise of mobile apps that deep linking became a key part of the marketing landscape. In the early days of mobile apps, deep linking was primarily used for in-app messaging and user onboarding, allowing marketers to guide users through the app and highlight specific features.

In recent years, deep linking has become a more sophisticated technique, with the introduction of technologies like deferred deep linking and contextual deep linking. These technologies allow marketers to link users directly to specific pages or features within an app, even if the app is not currently installed on the user's device.

Some of the pioneers in deep linking marketing include companies like Branch Metrics, which was founded in 2014 and has become a leader in the deep linking space. Other notable companies in this field include Firebase (now part of Google), Button, and Branch.io.

deep linking marketing has evolved significantly over the years, from its early roots in in-app messaging to its current form as a key part of the mobile marketing landscape. As the use of mobile devices continues to grow, deep linking is likely to remain an important technique for driving user engagement and improving the mobile user experience.

Affiliate marketing has been around for several decades, long before the advent of the internet. It originated in the 1980s, when businesses would pay commissions to salespeople for referring customers to their products or services. This model was eventually adapted to the internet in the mid-1990s, with the emergence of e-commerce websites like Amazon and CDNow, which offered affiliate programs to incentivize third-party websites to promote their products.

The internet fundamentally changed affiliate marketing by making it more accessible and scalable. With the ability to track clicks and sales in real-time, businesses could more easily measure the effectiveness of their affiliate programs and make data-driven decisions about how to optimize them. The rise of search engines and online advertising also created new opportunities for affiliate marketers to drive traffic and sales through paid channels.

Social media has also had a significant impact on affiliate marketing, particularly with the rise of influencer marketing. Influencers can use their social media platforms to promote products and services to their followers, earning a commission for any resulting sales. Social media has also made it easier for businesses to identify and recruit affiliate partners, and for affiliates to share their affiliate links with their audience.

The evolution of affiliate marketing has been shaped by technological advancements and changes in consumer behavior. As digital channels continue to evolve, it's likely that affiliate marketing will continue to adapt and evolve to remain a valuable tool for businesses looking to drive sales and revenue.

Deep linking marketing, affiliate marketing, and attribution marketing are related concepts in the broader field of digital marketing, but they are not the same thing.

Deep linking marketing is a technique that allows marketers to link directly to a specific page or feature within an app, rather than just the app's homepage. This technique can be useful for driving user engagement and improving the user experience by making it easier for users to access specific content within an app.

Affiliate marketing, on the other hand, is a type of performance-based marketing in which an affiliate promotes a product or service and earns a commission for each sale or conversion they generate. Affiliates typically use a unique affiliate link to promote the product or service, and the link is tracked to ensure that the affiliate receives credit for any sales or conversions they generate.

Table 2 - Attribution Platforms

Attribution Platform	Key Features/Differentiators
Google Analytics	Google Analytics offers robust attribution modeling capabilities, allowing marketers to analyze and optimize the performance of their digital marketing campaigns. Google Analytics also integrates with Google Ads and other Google products, making it easy to track and measure the impact of various channels on conversions.
Adobe Analytics	Adobe Analytics provides comprehensive cross-channel attribution capabilities, allowing marketers to track user behavior across devices and touchpoints. Adobe Analytics also offers advanced predictive modeling and machine learning capabilities to help marketers identify high-value customer segments and optimize marketing campaigns.
Kochava	Kochava is a mobile attribution platform that offers real-time attribution tracking across multiple channels and ad networks. Kochava also provides advanced fraud detection capabilities and granular data visualization tools, making it a popular choice for mobile app marketers.
Branch	Branch is a mobile deep linking and attribution platform that offers a wide range of attribution and measurement capabilities, including support for cross-channel attribution and real-time campaign analytics. Branch also provides advanced deep linking capabilities to help drive app installs and engagement.
Adjust	Adjust is a mobile attribution and analytics platform that provides real-time attribution tracking, fraud prevention, and audience segmentation capabilities. Adjust also offers advanced in-app event tracking and automation capabilities, making it a popular choice for mobile app marketers.
Singular	Singular is a cross-channel attribution platform that offers real-time attribution tracking and advanced ROI reporting capabilities. Singular also provides extensive fraud detection and prevention features, making it a popular choice for advertisers looking to ensure the integrity of their campaigns.

Attribution marketing is a broader concept that refers to the process of tracking and measuring the effectiveness of marketing campaigns across multiple channels and touchpoints. Attribution marketing involves assigning credit to each touchpoint in the customer journey to determine which channels and campaigns are most effective at driving results.

While these concepts are related, they each involve different techniques and strategies for achieving marketing goals. Deep linking marketing can be used in conjunction with affiliate marketing and attribution marketing to improve user engagement and track the effectiveness of marketing campaigns, but it is not the same thing as these other concepts.

Attribution platforms are tools that help businesses track and measure the effectiveness of their marketing campaigns across multiple channels and touchpoints. They work by assigning credit to each touchpoint in the customer journey, from initial ad impression to final purchase or conversion, to determine which channels and campaigns are most effective at driving results.

Attribution platforms can be valuable for businesses looking to optimize their marketing efforts and make data-driven decisions about where to invest their marketing budgets. They can help businesses understand the impact of different marketing channels and tactics, as well as identify areas for improvement in their campaigns.

Businesses in a wide range of industries use attribution platforms, including e-commerce, retail, finance, and more. Influencers may also use attribution platforms to track the success of their sponsored content and demonstrate the value they bring to their clients.

Attribution platforms can be a powerful tool for businesses looking to optimize their marketing efforts and make data-driven decisions. However, it's important to choose the right platform for your business needs and to understand the limitations of attribution modeling. Additionally, attribution platforms require careful implementation and ongoing maintenance to ensure accurate tracking and measurement of marketing campaigns.

Reputation Management is the practice of monitoring and shaping public perception of an individual, organization, or brand. It involves tracking what is being said about the entity on various online and offline platforms, responding to negative comments or reviews, and taking proactive steps to promote a positive image. Reputation Management is closely related to marketing because it involves building and maintaining a positive image for a brand or individual, which is crucial for attracting and retaining customers or supporters. Reputation Management is often considered a subset of Public Relations (PR) because it involves managing the public perception of an entity.

Reputation Management is not the same thing as Attribution Marketing. Attribution Marketing is a method of measuring the effectiveness of various marketing channels and campaigns in terms of driving conversions or sales. It involves tracking user behavior and interactions with different touchpoints along the customer journey, and attributing credit to the channels or campaigns that played a role in the conversion. Attribution Marketing is typically used to optimize marketing strategies and allocate budgets effectively. While Reputation Management can involve tracking metrics such as online reviews, social media mentions, and search engine results, its focus is on managing the public perception of an entity rather than measuring the effectiveness of marketing campaigns.

Knowing the etymology of words like "brand" and "branding" can help us understand their origins and evolution over time. This knowledge can provide us with valuable insights into the historical and cultural contexts in which these words emerged and the meanings and associations that they carry.

In the case of "brand" and "branding," understanding their origins as terms used in the context of marking livestock with hot irons can help us appreciate how the concept of branding has evolved and expanded to encompass a wide range of meanings and associations. It can also help us understand the symbolic and cultural significance of branding in modern society, where it is used to communicate messages about identity, quality, and value to consumers.

In addition to providing historical and cultural context, knowing the etymology of words can also help us improve our communication skills by enabling us to use words more effectively and precisely. By understanding the roots and meanings of words, we can choose words that are more appropriate and impactful in different contexts, and we can use words more creatively and innovatively to express new ideas and concepts.

The word "brand" comes from the Old Norse word "brandr," which means "to burn." Originally, branding referred to the practice of marking livestock with a hot iron to indicate ownership. Over time, the term "brand" came to be associated with the specific symbols or marks used to indicate ownership and quality of products.

The concept of branding as we know it today emerged in the late 19th and early 20th centuries with the rise of mass production and mass advertising. Companies began to recognize the importance of creating distinct identities and personalities for their products in order to stand out in crowded markets and build customer loyalty.

One of the earliest examples of modern branding is Coca-Cola, which began using its signature logo in the late 19th century and created a distinct visual identity and marketing strategy that helped it become one of the world's most recognizable brands.

In the early 20th century, branding continued to evolve with the emergence of radio and television advertising, which allowed companies to reach larger audiences and build even stronger brand identities. Over time, branding became a critical aspect of marketing and business strategy, with companies investing significant resources in developing and maintaining their brand identities.

Branding is an essential aspect of marketing and is used by companies of all sizes and industries to differentiate themselves from competitors, build customer loyalty, and create value for their products and services.

One famous book that explores the relationship between marketing, word choice, and etymology is "Words that Sell" by Richard Bayan. This book provides a comprehensive list of powerful words and phrases that can be used in marketing and advertising to evoke emotion and persuade customers.

Another book that touches on the importance of word choice and diction in marketing is "The Elements of Style" by William Strunk Jr. and E.B. White. While not specifically about marketing, this book is a classic guide to clear and effective writing that can be applied to any kind of communication, including marketing and advertising.

In terms of famous quotes related to this topic, one that stands out is from advertising pioneer David Ogilvy:

> *On the average, five times as many people read the headline as read the body copy. When you have written your headline, you have spent eighty cents out of your dollar.*

The quote highlights the importance of **choosing the right words** and phrasing in headlines and titles, which can have a significant impact on how many people engage with your content.

Another famous quote related to the importance of word choice in marketing comes from branding expert Walter Landor:

> *Products are made in the factory, but brands are created in the mind.*

This quote emphasizes the importance of using language and imagery that creates a clear and compelling brand identity in the minds of consumers.

"Bad news travels at the speed of light; good news travels like molasses." - John Jantsch

Branding is the process of creating a unique identity and image for a company, product, or service in the minds of consumers. It involves developing a distinct personality, values, and visual identity that differentiate a company or product from its competitors. Branding is essential for businesses because it helps create customer recognition, loyalty, and trust. Strong branding can help companies stand out in crowded markets, increase customer engagement, and drive sales.

"The key to successful crisis management is not good vs. bad, it's preventing the bad from getting worse." - Andy Gilman

If a brand is tarnished, it can have significant negative consequences for a business. A tarnished brand can lead to decreased sales, loss of customer loyalty and trust, and reputational damage that can take years to repair. This can happen for a variety of reasons, such as a product recall, a public relations crisis, or negative reviews or press coverage.

Some famous case studies of brands that have had to navigate through a tarnished image and reputation include:

1. Tylenol - In 1982, seven people died after taking Tylenol capsules that had been laced with cyanide. The incident led to a massive product recall and significant reputational damage for the brand. Johnson & Johnson, the parent company of Tylenol, responded by quickly recalling all products, introducing tamper-proof packaging, and launching a major public relations campaign to reassure customers and rebuild trust in the brand.
2. Volkswagen - In 2015, Volkswagen was caught cheating on emissions tests for its diesel vehicles. The scandal resulted in a $14.7 billion settlement and significant damage to the brand's reputation. Volkswagen responded by launching a series of ads that acknowledged the mistake, apologized to customers, and promised to make things right.
3. Pepsi - In 2017, Pepsi launched an ad featuring Kendall Jenner that was widely criticized for trivializing political protests and social justice issues. The ad was pulled, and Pepsi issued an apology for the tone-deaf campaign.

In general, companies can navigate through tarnished reputations by taking swift and decisive action, acknowledging the issue, and taking steps to make things right. This might involve apologizing to customers, offering refunds or compensation, and making significant changes to the product or service. It's also important to communicate openly and honestly with customers and stakeholders and to demonstrate a commitment to transparency and accountability.

Marketing has always been an integral part of any successful business. In today's rapidly changing economy, it is more important than ever for businesses to stay on top of the latest marketing trends and techniques to remain competitive. The world of marketing is constantly evolving, and the use of technology and data analytics is rapidly transforming the industry.

This book explores the different facets of marketing, from traditional marketing techniques to the latest digital marketing strategies. It provides insights into how marketing can be used to improve customer experiences, build brand loyalty, and drive business growth.

The author, Toni Urrutia, is passionate about marketing and has extensive experience in the field. He has created open-source educational resources (OERs) on marketing, which are available on her website, toniurrutia.com/oer, and has published this book to share her knowledge and insights with a wider audience.

This book is a work in progress and is being published in its current form for the KDP and Kindle audience only to raise funds for certain projects, which can be viewed on Toni Urrutia's website, toniurrutia.com/projects. The author encourages readers to visit her website for additional resources on marketing.

Marketing is an ever-evolving field that requires a deep understanding of the business being marketed and its position in the market and greater economy. The most successful marketers are those who remain adaptive to the rapidly changing marketing landscape and who are constantly exploring new techniques and strategies.

More and more, marketing involves "baking in marketing" into the product itself, which often entails automating the marketing process. This requires marketers to be tech-savvy and to keep up with the latest technological advancements.

Ultimately, good marketing is about creating a positive customer experience and building brand loyalty. By understanding the needs and desires of customers, marketers can create effective marketing campaigns that resonate with their target audience and drive business growth.

We hope this book has provided readers with valuable insights into the world of marketing and has inspired them to explore new marketing techniques and strategies. Remember, marketing is an art as well as a science, and the most successful marketers are those who can strike the right balance between the two.

The 2nd edition of "The State of Marketing: Customer Psychology, Technology, and Art" aims to provide readers with an updated and comprehensive view of the ever-changing landscape of marketing. This edition includes a range of new resources and features to help marketers stay on top of the latest trends, techniques, and technologies. Here is an overview of what readers can expect to find in the 2nd edition:

Primary Source Interviews: The 2nd edition includes interviews with prominent marketing experts and leaders in various industries. These interviews provide insights into their marketing strategies, approaches, and tactics, offering readers a unique perspective on marketing from those who are leading the way.

Appendix: The appendix provides a wealth of additional information and resources for readers. It includes a glossary of key marketing terms, a list of commonly used acronyms, and a directory of marketing associations and organizations.

Index: The index is a comprehensive guide to the contents of the book, making it easy for readers to quickly locate specific topics, concepts, or examples.

Resources: The resources section includes a range of additional tools and materials to help readers deepen their understanding of marketing. These include OERs (open-source educational resources), directories of companies and historical events, and links to top marketing websites and apps.

Proper Nouns: The proper nouns section includes a list of important people, brands, companies, and products mentioned throughout the book. This list helps readers keep track of key players in the marketing world and provides a reference for further research.

Real-time Resources: The real-time resources section includes a range of up-to-date information and tools to help readers stay on top of the latest marketing trends and techniques. These include curated real-time streams of news and information, links to top marketing apps, and directories of marketing companies and resources.

Apps: The apps section includes a list of top marketing apps, providing readers with tools to help them automate and streamline their marketing processes.

Curated Real-time Streams: The curated real-time streams section includes links to top marketing news and information websites, as well as social media accounts and blogs. These resources provide readers with up-to-date information on the latest marketing trends and techniques.

Topical Links: The topical links section includes links to top marketing resources organized by topic, such as SEO, social media, and content marketing. These links provide readers with additional information on specific marketing areas.

Prominent Figures: The prominent figures section includes profiles of top marketing leaders and experts, providing readers with insights into their backgrounds, experiences, and strategies.

Internal Links: The internal links section includes links to other sections of the book, allowing readers to easily navigate to related topics and content.

External Links: The external links section includes links to relevant resources and materials outside of the book, such as websites, blogs, and articles. These links provide readers with additional information and context on specific marketing topics.

The roadmap for the 2nd edition of "The State of Marketing" aims to provide readers with a comprehensive and up-to-date view of the marketing landscape. The new resources and features included in this edition are designed to help marketers stay on top of the latest trends and techniques, while also providing them with the tools and information they need to succeed in their marketing efforts.

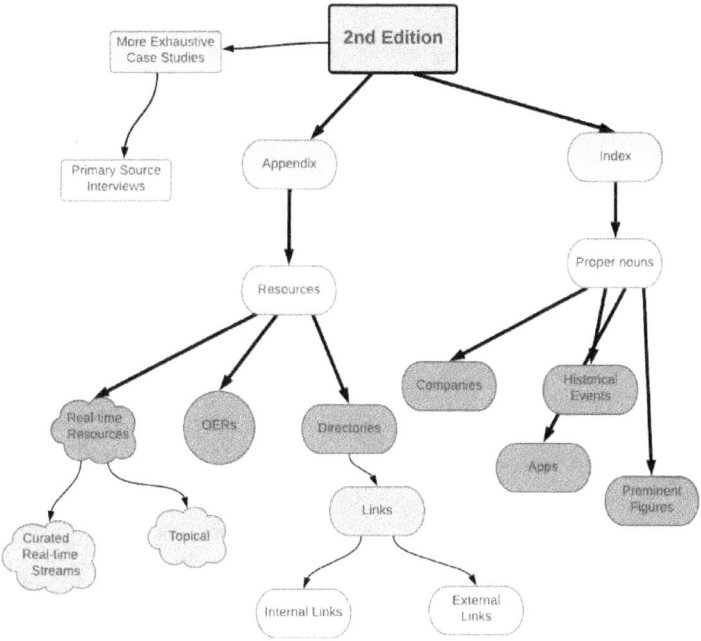

Figure 3 - 2nd Edition Roadmap